My Journey

Joann Sipes

MY JOURNEY
Copyright © 2023 by JOANN SIPES. All rights
reserved.

The opinions expressed by the author are not
necessarily those of Stonehenge
Literary and Media.

1846 E Innovation Park Dr STE 100 Oro Valley, AZ
85755
1-855-674-2878 | info@stonehengeliterary.com

Stonehenge Literary and Media is committed to
excellence in the publishing
Industry.

Published in the United States of America

ISBN: 978-1-0881-0843-7
eISBN: 978-1-0881-0851-2

Forward:

I met Joann and her husband when they began attending Rollins Christian Fellowship Church in Manton, Michigan. I knew right away that she would be a wonderful friend, encourager, prayer partner, and worker. Her love for the Lord was so contagious, and her gift of teaching children was amazing. She gave the devotions in our AWANA Clubs for years, and I was privileged to help lead the children to the Lord who made decisions during our Council Time. Joann is also remarkably creative in her art and sewing, and has helped us designing backgrounds for our Christmas drama, costumes, and a host of other projects. She always has a ready smile, enjoys humor, and teasing her husband, John.

As you read Joann's testimony and her journey through life, you will be reminded over and over how God is faithful in bringing her through times of joy, suffering, and pain.

"Great is Thy faithfulness" Lamentations 3:23

My Journey

By Joann Sipes

If you are reading this, it is because God has opened the door for me to write this short book in hopes it will speak to someone else during their life journey. Maybe that person is you. It is my prayer that my story will be a blessing to all who read it. And you will see through my testimony, God is real and He works through situations and people to accomplish His will in our life and He knows what is best for us.

As I remember happenings from my life, I know God was with me through the mountain top experiences as well as the valleys. He has never failed me, though I have failed Him many times. He has always been there for me even when I didn't know Him in a personal way. God is there for you as well, whether you realize it or not.

(Joann at 2 years old)

I was adopted at twenty-three months with one pair of holey training pants, and impetigo over two thirds of my body. My natural mother could no longer care for me, and through a friend found a couple who wanted children and could not conceive. My mother asked this couple to take me, and they jumped at the chance. My future mom made me a bunch of clothes, took me to the doctor, and in time I was healed. Then my natural mom took me back. Within a short time, she called my future mom and asked her to take me once again. This time my future mom replied, "No! Not unless you sign papers." My natural mom told me I had cried for a week for mashed potatoes and she couldn't handle having me any longer.

(My mom, dad, and me when I was 3 years old)

The papers were legally signed and I had a home that loved me. Mom and Dad were good moral people but strict. I grew up knowing my limits and respecting my elders. I knew when mom said to mind that I'd better mind, but once in a while I would get in trouble with some of my cousins.

(The house I grew up in)

I do remember an older couple that lived next door to us. I called them grandma and grandpa Haggy. They were so sweet when I would go visit with them. There was something special about Grandma Haggy. She was always so kind and took time to visit with me no matter how busy she was. One day, she had Grandpa help her clean out the old shed behind their house. I wondered why. Then she invited my cousin April and me to play in the new play house they had fixed up so we could have a tea party. She would bring out cookies and tea for us to enjoy. April and I were very young.

Grandpa Haggy grew Hungarian hot peppers behind the play house. He had some very black dirt delivered to his back yard. Mom and aunt Marj had just given April and me a bath and put pretty lace dresses on both of us. They planned to take us to some party, and told us we could go outside while they got ready, and to stay clean as we would be leaving soon. Well, that huge mound of dirt was just too much of a temptation, and we began sliding down that mound. Our beautiful dresses were ruined. We both were in trouble and needed a second bath. I don't remember whether we ever went to that party or not.

I remember faintly mom telling me to stay with her in a store when my cousins were running all over. Mom simply picked me up, and applied her hand of knowledge to my seat of learning. I had on a thick snowsuit with thick snow pants and didn't feel anything, but even as a child I was truly embarrassed, and never disobeyed her in the store again.

I was very small when mom and dad took me to church one Sunday. Apparently, I slid under the pews so mom and dad never took me back. I have often wondered as I think back, if someone would have come and invited them back to church, I might have heard about Jesus a lot earlier in life.

Over all, I had a good early child hood. I remember when I was five years old being very lonely except when my cousins came over. One memory I have is making mud pies on the back porch and talking to my invisible friend about good and bad. I knew in my heart good should win over bad. I'm not sure if I got that idea from the new TV we had or not. We watched a lot of Lone Ranger programs where the good guys always wore white hats and the bad guys always wore black. The good guys always won. At the time, I couldn't figure that out, but I remember feeling as I grew up that something was missing in my life.

(Kindergarten picture).

I remember my first day in Kindergarten. Mom had me all ready and I caught the bus to school. When I got there, I was told I wasn't enrolled. Mom didn't drive, so I had to stay the whole day in the wrong school. It was scary for me as the teachers didn't know what to do with me. After that, Mom made arrangements for the neighbor girl, Irene, who was in the twelfth grade to walk me to school. Since there were no busses available for us, the two of us walked the three quarters of a mile to and from the school. Irene was also my baby setter and I just loved her. We all went out on the playground at the same time from kindergarten to senior high. One time I saw a twelfth-grade boy making fun of Irene. That made me mad, and as he ran by me, I stuck my foot out and tripped him right into a mud puddle! I then jumped on his stomach while he was on the

7

ground and began pounding on him. This poor boy was laughing so hard he couldn't do anything. By this time, kids were gathering all around. Irene grabbed me off the boy and walked me out into the play yard before the playground teacher got there. That afternoon, when she walked me home, she told mom what happened and everyone had a big laugh.

(My sister Carol & me)

When I turned nine years old Mom sat me down to tell me I had a sister who would be coming to live with us. Carol was my natural half-sister. She was eleven years old and I was going to meet the sister I never knew I had. I was beyond excited, and I told mom that everything I had would belong to my sister, too. Carol had a lot of problems when she came to live with us. We learned that the court was going to take her away from our natural mother if she didn't give her up. So my eleven-year-old sister called my mom and asked her if they would adopt her also. I felt so protected from the things my sister had to go through. Thankfully, she was able to finally settle in and our natural mother began to visit occasionally.

(Florence, my natural Mother)

Some of my cousins came to visit shortly after my sister was adopted into our family. I thought one cousin, Sammy, was a brat, but we usually got along. One time he took a switch off our huge willow tree in the back yard and began hitting my sister with it. That was my sister and I was mad. I grabbed the switch and began whipping him with it. He ran into the house crying. Mom called me in and asked me why I was whipping Sammy. After telling her what happened, the grownups told Sammy he got what he deserved, and told me I should not do that again. I did fight with my sister as all siblings do, but I didn't want anyone to bully my sister, as I would defend her and make sure they would regret it. I remember in school my sister would talk too much. One time, Mr. Tower, our teacher, had her come up front, bend over, and he hit her with his hand. I stood up and told Him he was wrong, and I hated him for making her bend over in a skirt, and hitting her with his hand. I was sent to the office. The principal asked why I was sent to the office as I never got in trouble, and when I told him, he put the teacher on report. I was glad I had my sis, but something was still missing in my life and I didn't know what it was.

A church group bought the strawberry farm on the corner near our house. Mom started letting us go to church as we could walk there, and we joined the youth group. It was nice, but it still left me feeling empty and that something was still missing in my life. All I was learning was what I should and should not do. Church was mostly a social thing. I continued to go even after the church moved to a new location. It was a good place to have fellowship with my friends. I never once heard anything about Jesus, and what He did for me to save me from my sin. All I got out of it was be good. If a preacher came too close to talking about a relationship with God he was gone within the month.

(John the Marine)

I met John after his discharge from the Marines. I was 16 and he thought I was five years older. The uniform made me take a second look. He liked me right away. Mom wasn't happy with me going with someone so much older, so they closely monitored us and things worked out. John and I fell in love. He came one day, and asked my Mom if He could marry me. He even showed her the ring he bought. She said he needed to talk to dad. Dad agreed to let us get married if I would finish my last year of high school. I was seventeen when we were married at the church I attended as a teen. That was June 27,1964

(We converted my wedding dress to a prom dress).

(Graduation picture).

In June, 1965, I graduated from High school and went a year to college. I was so happy that just before graduation I found out I was three months pregnant with our first child. We figured since I would only be 4 months along, I wouldn't show at graduation with the robes we had to wear. By this time, my sister Carol had quit school and was going with a young man that was in a lot of trouble with the law. He ended up in prison, and Carol found another young man who had gotten out of prison and was changing his life around for the better.

When I was about three months pregnant, John took me out to see an uncle on my natural family side and we went out poaching fish in a river next to a cornfield. It had rained that day, and the cornfield was very muddy. We had to hike quite a distance through the cornfield to get to the river. My legs started hurting as the mud gathered around my feet. Finally, I decided to go back to the truck and wait for them. The Conservation employee followed us most of the way home, and we were all very concerned, as we had fish out of season in the back of the truck. As we got near the house where my uncle lived, it started to rain harder and the road was turning to ice, so we decided to stay overnight at his home. During the night I began to have severe cramps and wanted to go to the hospital, but John said it was too dangerous out and wouldn't take me. I lost my precious baby that night. On my next visit to the doctor a month later, we found out I was still carrying my dead baby. I was devastated. John didn't seem to understand how I felt - like he didn't even care. I was devastated over that as well, but wanted to make our marriage work as I loved him so much. I knew he just couldn't understand what I was going through.

Our first home was in Holly, Michigan. It was a three-bedroom, brick home, with a full basement. I loved it. John's brother Dar decided to live with us. No one asked if it was alright with me, he just moved in. As far as Dar was concerned, I could do nothing right. I came home from school one day and had a burnt roast, vegetable, potatoes and gravy waiting for me. Dar kept telling me how much better of a cook he was than me. Since the pan was burnt from the roast, I asked John's brother how he made the gravy. He replied that he got it from a can in the cupboard and showed me the can. It said, Dog Food with Gravy. Apparently, His thumb was over the words "dog food" and all he saw were the words, gravy. Guess that dog food tasted pretty good. Not long after we moved into a trailer in Flint. That was fine with me as it was closer to John's work. He worked for General Motors at the Chevy plant, and I had gotten a job in a restaurant called Lum's of Florida. They sold hotdogs and beer. We were there a few months before moving next door to my parents. I talked John into going to a small Baptist church in Grand Blank. Unfortunately, that was the worst sermon I ever heard. The man was not a speaker, but he explained all the points of the Gospel in his message. That was the first time I really heard about the love of Jesus and how He gave His life and rose again to pay for my sin, and that I could receive Him as my Savior, and be sure of a home in Heaven. I got up out of my seat that morning, and went forward to pray and receive Jesus as my personal Savior. John asked me what I was doing, and I told him, "I'm going forward." After I prayed, I felt so free as I found what had been missing in my life. At that point, I began praying for the salvation of my parents and sister. I also asked God to save my husband as I knew he had been raised to believe Christianity was for the weak and that God is dead.

By this time, Carol married a young man named Carl. He had just gotten out of prison and was trying to change his life around. They had a daughter and another one on the way when we got the call that Carl had been in a bad accident. Apparently, a truck had run head on into his parked truck and threw him on top his steering wheel. His spleen was crushed, and he died shortly after.

Not long after that, mom started going to the small Baptist Church that bought the old church building on the corner. The old church moved out and built a bigger church a few miles away. This new church preached the Gospel and gave an invitation every Sunday. One Sunday, Mama accepted the Lord. That was one prayer answered.

(Carol after she returned home)

Carol was in an accident a year to the day after Carl died. She was drinking and driving when the man she was with started having chest pains. He grabbed the wheel and she lost control going around a curve. She ended up crashing into a tree. The man she was with died instantly. Carol's front car seat landed in the back of the car when it wrapped around the tree and pinned her inside. A doctor who lived in the area was able to amputate her leg to get her out of the car. We were only allowed to visit her, one person at a time, for five minutes on the hour. It was so hard seeing my sis like that. I was just a new Christian, but I knew she wasn't, so I prayed and asked God to save her life and that she too would trust in Jesus to be her Savior. Slowly Carol got better. They put her in a nursing home for rehabilitation. I would go visit her as often as I could. One day I walked in to see

Carol and she was very irritated and nervous. When all the nurses left, she told me the reason. Apparently, she had a roommate that was quite ill and had just passed away. Carol told me the nurses and a doctor came in and withdrew something from the other lady and then put it into her IV. A few seconds later the lady was dead. When they saw Carol was not sleeping, they told her not to tell anyone what she had seen. My poor sis was so scared. and even though she was close to getting out, we couldn't move her.

Daddy took a little longer to receive Jesus as his Savior than mom. He would tinker around in his garage a lot so when the pastor would come to visit, he would have to go visit dad in the garage. When daddy's birthday came up, I made him a card and wrote him a poem called "Daddy". It went like this:

As she sat on those steps of dreary grey, she bowed her head to humbly pray.
 "Dear Lord you know, just a child am I."
As she poured out her heart, she started to cry.
 "My daddy is a very wonderful man, but the sad thing is,
Why won't he let Jesus save, that poor lost soul of his?
 Oh, I love my daddy, and I hope and I pray,

He'll kneel down and ask Jesus into his heart
today."
  As she finished her prayer, and wiped her eyes,
Daddy came home with such a surprise.
 "I've found something special," he said with a
grin,
"It's something real special, that brings peace
within.
  We'll all go to church this Sunday and sing,
'Glory to God, our Savior and King!"
I've found what's been missing,
and now it's so clear,
Your prayers have been answered,
My child so dear.
                    by Joann Taylor Sipes

Mom told me that was the only time she saw
daddy cry when he read the poem. That week the
pastor came to visit daddy in the garage and asked
him if he had ever been saved. He explained how
Jesus came to pay for our sins by dying on the
cross and how He came back to life conquering sin
and death. Daddy prayed and asked Jesus to
forgive his sin right there in that old dirty garage.
I was so excited! That was my second prayer
answered. I still continued to pray for my sister
and my husband.

John and I never went back to that church where
I was saved, but we started going to another one

where we had friends. I was baptized a short time later in a spring fed lake on a cool spring day. Our Christian friends really encouraged us to come to their church.

(Our girls - Marj & Dawn)

When we had been married about five years and had two beautiful girls, John quit his job and we moved to Lake City. I was so happy to move north, and away from all the disruptions of family and friends demanding John's time and money. I wanted to have more time alone with my little family and husband so we could grow closer together, and have money to pay bills.

After we moved into a motel in Lake City. We found a home to rent on Houghton Lake. It was drafty and cold. Bats lived in our attic. While we were there, I got pregnant for our son Bryan. When he was 4 months old, he ended up in the hospital with pneumonia. After he got well, we were able to move into a cobblestone house in the country.

John worked at various jobs trying to make ends meet. His legs were getting very bad. While he was in the Marines, they did surgery on his legs where they stripped out most out most of his veins. They wanted to give him disability when he got out of the service, but he refused. They did a terrible job on his legs and then made him hike before his legs were healed. By that time, he wished he would have accepted the disability as it was getting really hard to be on his legs a long time. We found a good home in Merritt, Michigan, and Dar helped build an addition on to our home. It was beautiful, but he kept charging John more than they had agreed on. We ran out of money, so it never did get finished. Meanwhile John's legs were getting so bad he filed for disability as he needed to have another surgery to strip the veins again in his legs. We ended up losing the house as we were fighting for the disability. By this time, I was working as a cook in a restaurant in Houghton Lake.

Before we lost our home, I was sitting in my chair one afternoon praying and asking God what he wanted me to do to serve Him. I was still fairly new at being a Christian, and wasn't sure how I could serve my Lord. I began to drift off to a semi state of sleep when I saw a vision. I saw several children coming through my front door. There was a measure on the wall. As the children came in, not one of them measured up. but when they left, they all measured up to the measurement on the wall. I realized then that God wanted me to reach unsaved children for the Lord. Still being a fairly new Christian, I asked God again if He would show me clearly that I was to reach unreached children for Him. Since I wanted to know for sure this was the right decision, I asked Him to show me by sending a white car to pass by me as I was traveling home on a lonely road. I didn't see any cars coming towards me or behind me, but as I got almost home, a white car passed me like I was sitting still and zoomed out of sight. To me that was the conformation I needed that God gave me. I was convinced then that this was my calling. I began going to Houghton Lake Baptist Church. I thought John was fine with me going. He even went with me sometimes. As I taught Sunday School and Junior Church, I really started to grow in the Lord because I had to get into God's Word to teach the children.

(Our son Bryan - 2 years old with his dad)

During this time, I was introduced to Child Evangelism Fellowship and taught a Good News Club in my home. I went to their weekly training as well. My son, Bryan, who was 3 years old at the time, looked at a picture of Jesus knocking on a door and told me "I want Jesus, my heart." What a joy for me when I was able to lead this little boy of mine to the Lord. He was hearing the good news of salvation three times a week, and I realized that when a child understands that he is a sinner and that Jesus took his place of punishment, then he can be saved. He has never forgotten that time, even though he fell away for a short period of time. He came back to the Lord and now lives for the Lord. I also was able to lead both of our girls to the Lord as well.

We finally moved to mom and Dad's farm they bought in Merritt, and fixed it up so they could be near us. The farm was cold and drafty. We had a wood stove that we slept next to so we could keep warm. I remember one Christmas when John forgot to turn the draft down on the stove and we woke up to a cherry red stove pipe. The chimney was on fire! We called the fire department and I got the children and pets out of the house. I grabbed the family Bible, and the kids Christmas gifts and we all went to the car. After the fire department put out the chimney fire, we found out the chimney had no liner. There was a crook in the chimney where the top half met the bottom half and bricks had fallen out. We were amazed that the whole house didn't burn down! John fixed that problem right away.

I was so concerned for my husband and my sister as they still had not yet accepted Jesus as their Savior. I prayed for them so often. I remember lying in bed one day praying for my husband as I told the Lord that "I didn't care what you have to do to me, but please help my husband ask Jesus to be his Savior." I didn't realize at the time what I was in for. All I knew was John was going through a lot since he was not able to work, his legs were getting worse, and our home life was getting very stressful.

I was teaching my sisters' girls about Jesus while visiting mom and dad down state one day, when Carol seemed interested. As Carol and I were talking, I gave her the Gospel and told her how she could ask Jesus to be her Savior. She went through the motions and prayed with me. I thought she meant it, but shortly after she told me that she had done that to make me happy, and wanted to go on living her life the way she wanted, and didn't want me to tell me what to do. I was devastated, but I didn't think I was telling her she had to do this, I only wanted to give her the opportunity. I kept praying she would someday make the right choice before it was too late.

One night I woke up from a deep sleep and I felt I had to write down some thoughts I was having, so I grabbed a pencil and paper and began to write the following poem.

I was sitting in my lofty place,
assured I would go there.
For I accepted Jesus Christ as my Savior fair.
I knew to heaven I would go but
one day as I rest,
Christ Jesus came to show me
What words cannot express.

25

He showed me just a glimpse of hell,
and in there was a child,
of whom the truth I did not tell
while here on earth a while.
The child looked up at me and cried,
tears streaming down his face,
"Why didn't you ever tell me of Jesus
and this place!"
I cried "Oh Lord, Did I do this?"
"Am I the one to blame?"
"Am I the one who should have reached
this child in your dear name?"

Our job is to go forth and reach those children
where ever they may
go
with the Gospel so clear they'll
understand
and salvation they can know.

After this poem came to me, I had a deeper
realization that when children can understand
they are sinners, and that Jesus took their place of
punishment on the cross so they could have their
sins forgiven, then they are responsible for that
knowledge. I felt the need and urgency to reach
all the children I could with the truth of God's
Word. I took extensive training and learned how

to teach them in a positive way that God loves them and wants them saved. Children are so special to the Lord. I was working at a restaurant in Houghton Lake, but I continued to have my weekly Good News Club and taught Junior Church. John became so frustrated and told me I either needed to give up Jesus or give him up. My world crashed in around me again. I couldn't give up my Jesus, though I realized John had been taught Christianity was for the weak and foolish. Jesus was the one who filled that void in my life, and gave me the purpose I had been searching for all my life, and I couldn't give Him up, but I didn't want to lose John either.

John left our home and went back to Flint to work for some shady people in construction. When he would come up to visit the kids, he threatened to take them so I would never see them again. I fell apart and decided that if I lost John and my kids, I might as well be with Jesus. That day I went to the store and bought a bottle of sleeping pills. After I put my three children to bed for the night, I took the whole bottle. I then called John and told him what I done and to come and get his children so they will be alright. A three-hour trip only took him two hours. I faintly heard him come in the door when I heard my oldest child outside my bedroom door asking her dad, "Is Mama going to die?" I realized then how foolish I was acting. Those words burned into my soul. John rushed me to the doctor who called an ambulance. The driver and his wife asked me if I was saved. I said "yes." Then they replied, "How you going to face God with what you have done?" At that point I cried out to God, and asked Him to forgive me for what I had done. I was released from the hospital the next day. A couple days later I received a note from John telling me he wanted to be saved. He told me that he must be an awful person to have driven me to do what I did. I picked him up and we went to our Pastor who led him to the Lord. I waited a week to make sure he really meant it before we got back together. God answered my prayer for him, and he has been the best husband a man could ever be!

Finally, we moved to Lake Ann and I got a job in a cherry sorting factory to pay for school clothes for the children. I had worked in quite a few jobs in small factories before. John stayed home and helped with the kids and kept the home going. He was now on disability for his legs and could no longer work at a regular job. He tried to work several times, but his legs swelled up and turned black and blue. The doctor gave him the news that he would lose his legs if he kept on working. It was so devastating for him not to be able to work, so we decided to trade jobs. I didn't mind working, and he was really good with the children.

I was working at a factory in Traverse City when we found out mom had lung cancer. Doctors kept taking so many tests on mom that it was three months before they decided to operate. When they first had diagnosed her, the spot was as tiny as a pencil dot, but by the time of the surgery, it had grown into her esophagus and they couldn't get it all. I felt they were milking her insurance and was so upset. She went through three years of radiation and a lot of medication to help keep the pain down before the cancer took her to heaven. Just a few weeks before mom died, she had a panic attack in the living room. Knowing mom had trusted Jesus as her Savior, I tried to reassure her that we would see her again. Mom answered, "I know I will see you, honey, but I won't see your sister Carol." At that point we were all crying, and Carol who was also with us, told me she wanted to ask the Lord Jesus to be her Savior. She really meant it this time. Mom was instantly at peace as my sis prayed and ask Jesus to be her Savior. Mom quietly went to be with the Lord a short time later.

Finally, after a couple more moves, we were able to build a beautiful three-bedroom home in Traverse City. I loved it but it was on a plateau. It had a walkout basement and a lot of room for storage. There were large picture windows overlooking a beautiful woodland landscape. Unfortunately, I was now having problems with my legs as well, and it was getting so hard for me to walk up and down our hill since I had gained so much weight from so many years of stress eating and had also had a skating accident where I tore a hole in my meniscus that was never fixed. I was told by the doctor that I could have knee replacements if I would lose weight, so I decided to go to a weight loss doctor and had vertical ring gastroplasty. After I lost the weight I had gained, I went back to the same doctors and they said I was too young for the surgery. All the doctor said he could do at this point, was to straighten my legs so they wouldn't bend. I was disgusted with all doctors by that time, as they hadn't told me the truth as far as I was concerned. I didn't even want to get out of bed most mornings because I knew the pain, I would be experiencing the minute I put my feet on the floor and stood up. I decided to apply for a disability that the Social Security doctor himself recommended to me, and was able to get that.

Meanwhile Daddy was going downhill physically and mentally. After several trips to the doctor, we found he had developed Alzheimer's. I remember daddy giving me a card for my birthday. He wrote on it that he loved me, and he was sorry for what I would be going through taking care of him. My Uncle Doc told me I should take over his care as I was the one who legally could. I didn't want to take away his freedom, but he was driving and having small accidents and living in filth. When I went down to see daddy, he was quite confused. I thought he was being looked after by family that lived close by, but I realized I was mistaken. I went to get him his pills one day and noticed some different ones in his bottle. When I found out they were downers and that they were probably causing him to be more confused I stepped in and convinced dad to move north. Uncle Doc told me not to let dad move in with us because Alzheimer's is so difficult. Instead of moving in with us, we arranged for dad to be in a foster care in Kingsley until we could get some training so we could learn how to take care of him. While dad was there, we received a call that he had fallen down a flight of stairs onto a brick floor. He was rushed to the hospital with a closed head injury. We got to the hospital, and a very harsh doctor told us we might as well go home and not stay around waiting for my dad to die, and that he could die right away, or three months from now. It wasn't what he said as much as the rude way he said it that made me hurt so bad. I wasn't waiting for him to die. I was waiting for him to get better so we could have him home with us and take care of daddy ourselves. As time went on, we were planning on how we could get some training. Then my daddy contacted pneumonia and the hospital transferred him to the nursing home part of the hospital. One of the nurses decided without reading his chart that dad needed exercise. She proudly told us how hard he tried to do all the exercises. John instantly confronted her for pushing him to exercise when he had pneumonia. Daddy smiled when he saw me come in his room and told me he loved me. He died later that night. I was so sad but knew daddy was now with mama in Heaven and I will see them both again. Still, it's so hard to know if he would have lived longer if he had been at our house. I was comforted to know he and mom had both received the Lord Jesus as Savior.

I was thrilled to find my natural mother also became a Christian before she went to be with the Lord. She came to me one day and told me she had accepted Jesus as her Savior and ask me to forgive her for wanting to abort me and for giving me away. I told her, "No I won't forgive you. I thank you for giving me life and finding a good home for me when you couldn't take care of me". I told her she could have had that back- street abortion but chose to follow the law at that time and give me life. For that I am grateful.

We sold our new home that we built in Traverse City, and bought a home where I could get around better. The house was over eighty years old in the little town of Manton. Even though the house was very old, the rooms were big and I could get around in the scooter I now had. We had planned to build again, but as I settled into bed that first night, I thanked God for a place to live where I could get around inside, and asked Him to please let this work for us so I wouldn't have to keep moving. I began painting and decorating a little at a time, which I could do. As we settled in, we found a nice church, Rollins Christian Fellowship Church, and the church family and community made us feel at home.

Pastor Lanning and his wife Nancy came to visit us. I loved them right away. Pastor introduced me to Child Evangelism Fellowship® in our area. I had lost contact with this ministry in all of our moves, and I was so happy to know they were still active and in the area. I ended up joining the committee and was able to help the local director, Beth, with teaching. She was such an inspiration to me. I took the Teaching Children Effectively™ training so I could help Beth teach Good News

Clubs. It wasn't long after, that I took the Instructor of Teachers™ class so I could help teach the TCE Classes. It was such a wonderful blessing working with Beth as a volunteer. When Beth let the committee know, she was going to get married and resign, the Lord brought Renee as our Director for a short time. She also got married and moved down state. Don took over as Director. Then Don left to go into another ministry and we were left without a director. In 2001 I stepped in to that temporary position to keep the ministry going. Everything was in disarray. I had to sort through every paper in the office and try to get some organizing done. I ended up going to the Children's Ministry Institute in Missouri for two six-week sessions and graduating in 2002. It was very intensive training, but so fulfilling. I then worked as the Director for five years in this chapter of Child Evangelism Fellowship®. There are seven counties in this chapter, and I was able with God's leading to have ministry in each of these counties. God was good, but my health was not doing so well. I had a sensitive colon according to the many doctors I had gone to. On top of that, I had gotten the flu, and spent one night throwing up blood, but didn't go to the doctor when the blood stopped and I was feeling better. After that I started having a bad case of acid reflux. I began taking all kinds of antacids, but nothing seemed to work very well. I even developed an allergic reaction to one of them. I found I would get some relief if I ate a little something when the acid was getting bad. That led to weight gain again as I was starting to eat all the time. I was still able to teach the devotions in our AWANA Club at my church, and worked five years in CEF before stepping aside due to my colon problems and acid reflux. I suffered with acid closing off my throat for several years being misdiagnosed by several doctors. Finally, I went to a doctor who sent me to a specialist. Here is the testimony I was able to share at my church.

<u>February 5, 2015</u>

When I first went to the doctor for my acid reflux problem, he sent me to another doctor in Traverse city. I told him about my weight loss surgery in the 80's so I could have a knee replacement. It all began with a skating accident years before that, and it had caught up with me. Doctors had told me they would do the surgery if I lost weight. After I lost weight, they said I was still too young. The weight loss surgery I had was called a vertical ringed gastroplasty. That's where they staple part of the stomach off vertically.

Later, I was able to get both knees replaced after we moved to Manton. Sometime after we moved to Manton, I got a bad case of the flu. I was throwing up violently and my stomach began to bleed. I figured it was just really irritated so when it stopped bleeding, I didn't feel the need to go to the doctor. Now I realize that was not a good decision. After that, I began to have really bad acid reflux problems. Many nights I would wake up gasping for air after the acid would shoot up into my throat closing it off. Since it was getting worse, I found myself sitting in this surgeon's office telling him about my problem. Tests were taken and showed I had a hole from the working side of my stomach to the side that had been stapled off. The doctor said I needed a revision that should solve my problem. I went through all the hoops I needed to go through except the colonoscopy. I was trying to get out of that. The doctor insisted that I have this done, and as a result, that's when he found stage 3 colon cancer. Within two weeks I had surgery to remove one third of my colon and was sent to the oncologist for chemo. The oncologist told me I had an 80% chance of it coming back without chemo and a 50% with chemo. I was on chemo twice a month for six months. At the end of my chemo, I tested out cancer free. Needless to say, the acid reflux problem had to be put on the back burner. Meanwhile I continued teaching AWANA Club devotions even with my stomach acid getting worse. Between the chemo and the acid reflux I eventually lost all my teeth. A little over two years later, I went back to my surgeon to see if I could have something done. After several tests and a scope, it was found I had two holes in my stomach going through to the unused part that was stapled off. I also had more erosion to my throat. I was told I needed surgery, but I would be at risk whether I had the surgery or not. I did all they required again, complaining that I shouldn't have to attend some of the monthly meetings that absolutely taught me nothing for the second time. I had planned I would have my surgery in time to be well before our AWANA Club started up, but God had other plans, and I had to give up my desires and trust God who knows what was best. God then laid it on my heart to get all the lessons ready for the year just in case. I had been trying to make a three-year plan for the Sparks, and a four-year plan for the T&T groups. I figured that way they would have a basic knowledge of the Bible by the time they were ready for our Junior High class. I knew I needed the surgery as I didn't even have to lay down to have acid shoot up into my throat. It happened once when I was counseling three little girls, and the look on their faces made me want to cry. I was thankful it didn't last long and I was able to tell them I was fine. By this time, I had been cancer free for almost three years. My doctor was concerned that I could die. I told him that I knew where I was going and I would either be praising the Lord in Heaven or serving Him here. Friday, September 5, 2014, I went in for what should have been a three-and-a-half-hour surgery. Instead, it took five and a half hours and my kidneys began to close down twice. The doctor told my husband I was the only one who wasn't fearful of the surgery. He said, "I wish I had her faith." The doctor was supposed to be out of town that weekend but he felt uneasy about leaving so he stayed around the hospital. It was a good thing God made him uneasy, because on Sunday, September 7th, I went in for another emergency surgery. Everything started falling apart. John was told I probably wouldn't make it. But I had a great group of prayer warriors praying for me. They told me I woke up combative and pulled out my respirator. I don't remember that part. What I do remember is waking up in a near windowless depressing room where I could have only my husband and children to visit with. The room and everyone in blue seemed evil to me. I was under so many drugs I wasn't myself. I could not understand why God had not taken me home as I was in so much pain even with the drugs. I knew it was going to be a long recovery as the doctor had to remove my stomach and leave everything unattached so it could heal, but I wasn't prepared for this. I had my mind set I would either die right away or have a successful surgery and do really great. I finally was moved to a cheerier part of ICU, and was glad I could at least have visitors now. My granddaughter, Amirah, bought me a radio and set it on the Christian station for me. That really did lift my spirit. I had my family bring me some yarn and supplies and I began making things that I gave to as many nurses as I could. Between my devotions, knitting, and the Christian radio station, I was able to be more positive. Because of the tube running down through my nose, (to keep me from choking to death) I could not go to a nursing home, so I would need to stay in the hospital several weeks until I could be put back together with no stomach. They transferred me to the third floor in a private room with a nice view. The doctor told me I was scheduled for surgery November third, so the countdown began. I embroidered a picture of Jesus in the operating room with a surgeon for my doctor, and I told him that Jesus would be in there with him when he operated. He loved it and thanked me several times after that. Pastor Bart brought me a great AWANA poster the leaders and kids made and signed. That really encouraged my spirits. I had John put it on the wall. That opened the door for me to witness to almost everyone. Some would remember AWANA when they were kids. Some remembered sending their kids to AWANA Club.

Others wondered what AWANA was. That opened a lot of wonderful conversations. I tried to be careful not to be pushy, but to share what God has done for me. I was happy to be in that room as I could listen to my Christian music all the time and hear some great sermons. Many of the nurses told me they liked coming in my room because of the upbeat Christian atmosphere. I was able to share my testimony with many of them including some doctors. I even had some of them ask for prayer for various things and situations. Many times, we would stop and say a quick prayer right there. Some even prayed for me. I set goals for myself and praised God as I was able to meet each goal. Doctors and nurses were amazed at how well I was doing and I made sure they knew God was my strength and that a lot of people were praying for me. After all, it is prayer and God that got me through. All this time I could not eat or drink anything by mouth. I will never take a drink of water for granted again! All my nourishment was through my feeding tube. I would pretend I was getting escalloped potatoes or some other good thing to eat every time they filled up my feeding bag. The nurses had a lot of fun asking me what I wanted for dinner each day. Finally, November third arrived and surgery went well to reconnect my esophagus with my small intestine. The doctor was out of town the next day when they wheeled me into surgery for another emergency. My feeding tube had fallen out during the night from where it was supposed to be, and I had to be opened up for my fourth major surgery in three months. Doctors told John again that I probably wouldn't make it. I woke up back in the same depressing room I was in after the first emergency operation. It was the room they put you in when they think you're going to die. This time they had my arms tied to the bed around my wrists and elbows so I couldn't pull the respirator out, or thresh around. Thankfully, they did take it out not long after that, and I could breathe and talk better. As I lay in that depressing gloomy room, I cried out to God and asked Him to please show me why I had to be in that awful place again. The very next day God answered my prayer. This time I had a sweet nurse who also enjoyed my Christian radio station. We talked about our faith as she would care for my needs. When she came by the next day, she asked me to pray for her son. She was a single mom trying to raise a twelve-year-old daughter and a fourteen-year-old son. He would go to church with her and was saved in AWANA, but began running around with some rebellious friends and was becoming rebellious himself. We held hands and prayed for her son together. I shared with her a testimony about a fourteen-year-old boy who hated the world and was in foster care with no mother or father. I told her how finding out how much God loved him he received

Jesus as his Savior. He had never felt loved before and it changed his life totally. I told her to never give up because she's a single mom, but to always pray for him and tell him how much she loves him whenever she can. It may take a while, but God will work in his life and bring him back. Her reply was, "Here you are so sick, and you are ministering to me." She thanked me and told me she would follow my advice and this her gave her hope. I realized then why I had to be in that room again. I know I am no one special, but God wanted to use me to encourage another Christian. I'm thankful for that. I was transferred to the better part of ICU the next day. I was grateful I had a window. Light would come in even though the view wasn't so great. The nurses all knew me from the last time and treated me really well. I was in the hospital so long by this time that I would find myself getting down and depressed at times. It seemed whenever I would start to feeling down, God would remind me of a verse, song, or bring in a nurse that would encourage me and lift my spirit up. Some of the nurses seemed to know when to come in, hold my hand, and pray with me. God was so good to me and gave me strength when I needed Him. My doctor came in to give me updates on how I was doing. The facts I could handle, but his opinion was usually negative and that would make me feel down. I wanted to give up and cried out to God asking Him what He wanted me to do. A short time later another doctor came in and assured me the leak we were concerned about would heal and I will improve. That lifted my spirit and gave me the hope I needed. The next time my doctor gave me an update I told him to please just share the facts as I know what they mean. I told him that a negative opinion only brought me down, and that I was even considering giving up, going home and calling in hospice, after the last negative opinion. I told him I needed something positive to hold on to. He kindly did what I ask after that. I finally had confidence in my doctor, and he was amazed at my progress. God knows exactly what we need. All we need to do is pray and trust Him to answer what is best for us. Just before sending me home, my doctor came in and told John and me that he was pleased at how I was progressing. He said, "nine out of ten people who go through what you have been through in this short period of time don't usually make it!" I answered, "That's because God doesn't want me in heaven yet. I still have His work to do." He agreed that I was probably right. I was sent home on November 28th, 2014, after being in the hospital eighty-four days. They changed my feeding to something different than I had in the hospital, and ran it at a faster speed. Another doctor insisted I take an antibiotic at home that I didn't think I needed as I had a good white blood count and no fever. She said I had to have the antibiotic or go to a nursing home if my family couldn't deal with it. After what my sister and dad had gone through, I wanted nothing to do with a nursing home. Not long after I got home, the antibiotic reacted and gave me the hives all over my body. I had huge welts, so we stopped the medicine and I took Benadryl instead. The hives wouldn't go away so John took me to Munson hospital to see if they could help me. After seeing a rude doctor and receiving no help, we went home. Dawn began to research everything I was being given. We found out that my food was keeping the hives going. We called the doctor's office and the nurse practitioner changed my food back to what I had in the hospital and cut down the speed. It was eight days of torture for me by the time I found relief. We were all praising God for that answer to prayer, and for that wonderful nurse. Every day after that I started doing better. I no longer needed my therapist or my nurses as I no longer had my wound vac. My drain fell out after the doctor cut it off. My drink test revealed the leak was almost gone. The doctor felt it had healed up now, which was an answer to prayer. I could eat soft pureed food and drink liquids. In fact, the Doctor had scheduled me for another drink test when I went to see him on Tuesday, Feb. 10, 2015, and I was able to get rid of the feeding tube. I was looking forward to that tube being taken out! I was also looking forward to continuing serving our Lord wherever He wanted me and where He opened the doors with my husband's blessing. I am so thankful for everyone who prayed, sent cards, flowers, encouragement and help, as my family and I had been going through all this. I learned to lean on God and trust Him, knowing that whatever He does will be for my good and His glory.

In September of 2015, I was accepted back in the Child Evangelism Fellowship Northwest Chapter. They had gone through an extensive make over as far as how it was run, but they stayed with the same Biblical teaching they always have had. Instead of being a director this time, I was so happy to become the Coordinator of the Northwest Michigan seven-county chapter. The job is the same, even though the title had changed.

My heart is in reaching boys and girls for the Lord. I thank the Lord for His grace and for watching over me all my life. I thank the Lord for my salvation. There are times I've been weak and let the Lord down, but He has never let me down.

I don't know what the Lord has in store for me for the future, but I do know He wants the best and that He always keeps His Word. He keeps His word to you as well. God works behind the scenes for our good, to accomplish His purpose in our lives. If I can be a blessing to others, and am given the opportunity to share the Gospel to the unsaved no matter how old or young, then I will have achieved the purpose God has for my life. Through the years, God has blessed me, and He will bless you as well when you accept His free gift of salvation only found in His Son, the Lord Jesus Christ. Jesus said, "... I am the way, the truth, and the life: no man cometh unto the Father, but by me." John 14:6 (KJV) We can't work our way to heaven.

The Bible says, "For all have sinned, and come short of the glory of God." We have all been born with the desire to have our own way and not God's way. Sin is anything that goes against God's laws. None of us are perfect like God, Romans 3:23 The bible also says, "For the wages of sin *is* death, but the gift of God *is* eternal life through Jesus Christ our Lord." In Romans 6:23, Death means separation from God forever. Not only here on earth but after the body dies, your spirit will also be separated from God forever in a place of torment. But because God loves you, He offers the gift of eternal life in Heaven with Him now, and when your spirit leaves your body. God gives each of us a choice, and only you can choose to believe on Jesus as your Savior. God never sends anyone to hell. They choose to go there by rejecting His gift of salvation. God's Word says, "That if thou shalt confess with thy mouth the Lord Jesus, and shalt believe in thine heart that God hath raised him from the dead, thou shalt be saved. For with the heart man believeth unto righteousness; and with the mouth confession is made unto salvation." Romans 10:9-10

"For whosoever shall call upon the name of the Lord shall be saved." Romans 10:13

"For by grace are ye saved through faith; and that not of yourselves: *it is* the gift of God: Not of works, lest any man should boast." Ephesians 2:8-9 We can't work our way to heaven, because none of us can be as perfect as God. We just have to believe and receive His free gift of salvation. But we do work for the Lord because we love Him, and want to live the Christian life He has planned for us. We have a desire to get to know Him better and become more like Jesus. Jesus will then live His life in us through His Holy Spirit. The Holy Spirit then helps us understand God's Word and gives us strength to live for Him if we let Him. When we do wrong or fail, God will forgive if we come to Him and confess our sin, and then we can have a closer relationship with our Lord. 1 John 1:9 says

"If we confess our sins, he is faithful and just to forgive us *our* sins, and to cleanse us from all unrighteousness." I know I have failed God, but He has never failed me. I have never met a person that was sorry they received God's gift of forgiveness. I hope and pray my story has been a blessing and gives you hope in the blessings God has for your life as well.

I'll end with this poem

God's Love

Oh, what love He has for us to shed His blood
upon the cross.
The pain of being beaten, and those thorns, His
brow embossed.
What great love that kept Him going through
such torture and such shame.
What a plan of great salvation, full of love and
full of pain.
What He said was pure divine. What mere
human could be so kind?
"Father, forgive them, for they know not what
they do."
"When He said it is finished." He gave salvation
to me and to you.

Oh the glory when the third day came and the
stone was rolled away
To reveal an angel sitting where Jesus used to

lay.

Yes, He's risen! Yes, He's risen! Now new life is a gift to all,

If only we want to be forgiven and we answer his great call.

He is standing at our heart's door knocking to come in.

His love is shown beyond compare. How will you answer Him?

by Joann Sipes

God gives you freedom to choose the Lord Jesus, and have everlasting life with Him in Heaven, or to choose to reject Jesus and have everlasting punishment in Hell, a place of torment. The choice is yours.

If you truly want to believe on Jesus as your Savior, just pray a sample prayer like this:

Dear Jesus, I believe you are the perfect Son of God. I know I'm a sinner, and that you died to pay for my sin, were buried, and rose again. Please come into my heart and make me your very own. Help me to live for you. In Jesus name, Amen

If you prayed a prayer like that and really meant it, you now belong to God and He will always be with you to help you understand His Word and help you live for Him. (Hebrews 13:5-6) We are going to stumble and fall at times, but God promises whenever we confess our sin to Him, He forgives our sin and makes everything new again. (1 John 1:9)

I'm so happy I found Jesus as my Savior!

Joann Marie Sipes

A note of thanks

I would like to thank my wonderful husband who has backed me completely in my ministry since he accepted the Lord Jesus as his Savior and who gave me his permission to write my story. He has been there for me and encouraged me to be my best and loved me at my worst. Thank you to my editor and all those who encouraged me to continue serving our Lord through the years. Most of all Thank you Lord Jesus for watching over me all my life, and never leaving me.

Hebrews 13:5

Printed in the USA
CPSIA information can be obtained
at www.ICGtesting.com
JSHW021003151023
50072JS00002B/79